PETERHOF

V. Sadovnikov. "The Great Cascade and the Great Palace in Peterhof". 1845

The Great Palace

The marble obelisk standing near the railing of the Upper Park in Peterhof bears the incised numbers *29,* which indicate the distance in kilometers from St Petersburg to the splendid suburban residence of the Russian Emperors and now a world-famous palace and park museum complex.

The idea of building a summer residence that would not be inferior to the famous Versailles of the French kings, occurred to Peter the Great in 1714. The Emperor himself supervised work on the design of fountains, palaces and parks. The French ambassador Campredon wrote to Louis XV that the progress in the construction of the new residence was "striking and amazing". Already on 15 August 1723 a ceremony of the inauguration of Peterhof ("Peter's court" in Dutch) took place. By that time some of the fountains were functioning, the decoration of the Upper Mansion and the construction of the Palace of Monplaisir

was over, and the Marly Palace and the Hermitage pavilion nearly completed. But on the whole, work on the creation of the ensemble contributed by such eminent architects as Le Blond, Niccolo Michetti, Francesco Bartolomeo Rastrelli, Yury Velten and Andrei Stakenschneider, continued for about two centuries.

The focal centre of of the ensemble is the Great Palace which towers above the edge of the 16-metre-high terrace. The three-storey stone building, flanked by two side wings surmounted with cupolas, was erected by Rastrelli in 1747–55. The architect reconstructed the building of the Petrine period and its austere design determined Rastrelli's restrained decoration of the façade of the central block. The further reconstruction of the palace executed by the architect Yury Velten dealt mainly with the interiors remade now in the style of Classicism which came to replace the Baroque.

3

In the eighteenth and nineteenth centuries the Peterhof Palace served as an official summer residence of the Russian Emperors. Its room and halls were witnesses to many major events. Festivals and receptions, balls and masquerades which gathered up to three thousand guests at the same time were held there.

The Great Palace is entered from the side of the Upper Park. The lavishly decorated gilded staircase leads to the no less luxurious Dance Hall – the first of the palace's state rooms. Next to it is the Chesme Room. The main decorative element in this room are twelve paintings by the German artist Philippe Hackaert illustrating the victory of the Russian Fleet over the Turks in Chesme Harbour.

The theme of the Chesme Battle is continued in the next, Throne Room, where the entire western wall is occupied by the four huge paintings of the English artist Richard Paton. These symbols of the naval glory of Russia are especially suited for Peterhof whose founder was the creator of the Russian Navy. The Throne Room is the largest room in the palace. Like the Chesme Room, it is decorated to the design of Yury Velten. Official receptions were generally held there. The dimensions of the hall, the streams of light pouring inside from twenty-eight two-tiered windows, the twelve beautiful chandeliers, the fine patterns of the parquet floor, the portraits of the representatives of the then ruling Romanov dynasty – all was intended to emphasize the significance of this room in a series of the ornate interiors of the palace. The main emphasis is laid on the eastern wall where the throne used to be installed. There hangs an equestrian portrait of Catherine the Great by the Danish artist Vigilius Erichsen, painted during the year of her ascent to the throne.

The small Audience Room, with its ceiling painting featuring a scene from Torquato Tasso's *Jerusalem Delivered* by the Italian artist Paolo Ballarini, was not altered by later refurbishments and has retained its magnificent Baroque decor of the middle of the eighteenth century. The Audience Hall, glistening with its rich gilded decor which is endlessly reflected in numerous mirrors, has been restored during the post-war period and produces no less beautiful impression than before.

After the Audience Hall with its luxury and glamour, the White Banqueting Hall, designed in the Classical style for formal dinners, evokes a feeling of calm and balance. Light shades are predominant in its decor and there are no paintings – the architect preferred high-relief compositions devoted to subjects from classical mythology. Displayed there is a faience service of 196 pieces commissioned by Catherine the Great from the famous English ceramist Josiah Wedgwood. The decoration of the table is enriched with Bohemian glass produced in the eighteenth century.

In the nineteenth century, during large receptions, tables were laid in the entire northern enfilade. As a memory of such feasts, at the opposite end of the suite of rooms there is another beautiful set, the Banqueting Service, decorated with a splendid flower design and manufactured at the Imperial Porcelain Factory specially for the Great Service.

The female apartments in the palace included the Boudoir, the Bedroom, the Dressing Room, the Study and a

The Main Staircase ▶

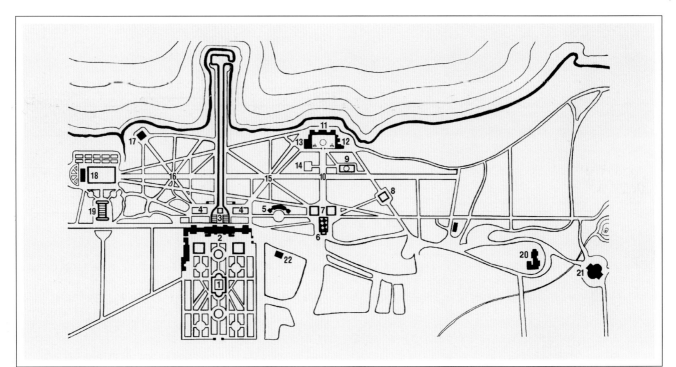

1. The Upper Gardens	8. The Pyramid Fountain	16. The Eve Fountain
2. The Great Palace	9. The Sun Fountain	17. The Hermitage Pavilion
3. The Great Cascade	10. The Monument to Peter the Great	18. The Marly Palace
4. The Bowl Fountains	11. The Palace of Monplaisir	19. The Golden Hill Cascade
5. The Orangery Pavilion and the Emperor's Tables Restaurant	12. The Bath House and the Assembly Hall	20. The Farm Palace
6. The Chessboard Hill Cascade	13. The Catherine Block	21. The Cottage Palace
7. The Roman Fountains	14. The Western Aviary	22. The Museum of the Benois Family
	15. The Adam Fountain	

The Throne Room ▶

The Ball Room

◀ The Ball Room

The Chesme Room

The Throne Room.
V. Erichsen. "Equestrian
Portrait of Catherine
the Great". 1762

The Blue Reception
Room. I. Aivazovsky
"View of the Great Palace
and the Great Cascade"

The Blue Reception Room

The Blue Reception Room. Vase.
The Imperial Porcelain Factory,
St Petersburg. Ca. 1830

The Audience Room.
J.G. Kirchner.
"St Wenzeslaus".
The Royal Porcelain Factory.
Meissen, Germany. Ca. 1730

The Audience Room.
Porcelain sculptures
on a console table.
The Royal Porcelain Factory,
Meissen, Germany.
Mid-18th century

*The White Banqueting Hall.
Items from the Husk Service.
The Etruria Pottery of J. Wedgwood,
Staffordshire, England. 18th century*

The White Banqueting Hall

The Blue Reception Room. V. Sadovnikov. "The Court Going Out of the Great Peterhof Palace"

number of service rooms, such as the Standard Room, the Cavaliers-in-Attendance Room, the Secretary's Room, etc. They are particularly interesting for their decor and art collections. The rooms owe much of their splendour to their wall decoration lined with silk in a variety of designs. As a rule these fabrics were first commissioned in Lyons, to be later imitated by Russian manufacturers. The colour and patterns of the wall linings are reflected in the second names of some apartments, such as the Large (Blue) Reception Room or the Boudoir (Partridge Drawing Room).

The two Chinese studies, the Eastern and Western Chinese Lobbies, invariably attract visitors' attention. The lacquered wall panels, the painted ceilings, the parquet floors inlaid with pieces of precious wood, the whimsically decorated ceramic stoves, the fabrics as well as the collections of Chinese and Japanese porcelain, enamels and furniture, all vividly introduces us into the exotic realm of the remote and mysterious countries.

In the central part of the palace, preserved during the reconstruction of the former Upper Mansion, there is a hall with two tiers of windows overlooking the flower parterre of the Upper Gardens and the Great Cascade with the Sea Canal in the Lower Park. During the Petrine Age this hall was the main and largest interior in the Upper Mansion. Later, after its reconstruction, on the orders of Catherine the Great, 368 paintings by the Italian artist Pietro Rotari were hung in the room and it began to be called the Picture Hall.

In this historical part of the palace there is also the famous Oak Study of Peter the Great. Its original decor executed by Jean-Baptiste Le Blond in the first quarter of the eighteenth century has mainly survived. The study is decorated with oak panels based on sketches by the well-known French decorator Nicolas Pineau. Their subjects deal with the flowering of sciences, arts and trade and eulogize the naval power of Russia.

One of the doors in the Picture Hall leads to the Oak Staircase, the main one in the palace. The staircase owes its name to the fancifully carved wooden rails. The portrait of Peter the Great in an ornate oak frame hanging on the wall reminds to the visitors of the museum once again about the outstanding reformer of Russia, the founder of St Petersburg and Peterhof.

The Western Chinese Lobby.
Incence-burner in the shape of duck.
China. Late 17th – early 18th century

The Western Chinese Lobby. Chinese
porcelain candlesticks. 18th century

◀ The Eastern Chinese Lobby. Stove with painted tile
decoration. Designed by J.-B. Vallin de la Mothe

The Western Chinese Lobby

The Partridge Drawing Room.
J.-B. Greuze. "Girl at the Table".
1760s

The Picture Hall.
Fireplace decoration:
"Volcano"

The Picture Hall

The Partridge Drawing Room

*The Picture Hall.
Porcelain sculptures
on a card-table.
The Royal Porcelain Factory,
Meissen, Germany.
Mid-18th century*

The Divan Room. H. Buchholz.
"Portrait of Elizabeth Petrovna
As a Child". Mid-18th century

The Divan Room

The Divan Room.
Porcelain sculpture: "Zemira".
By J. D. Rachette

The Divan Room.
Mirror in a porcelain frame.
The Royal Porcelain Factory,
Meissen, Germany.
Mid-18th century

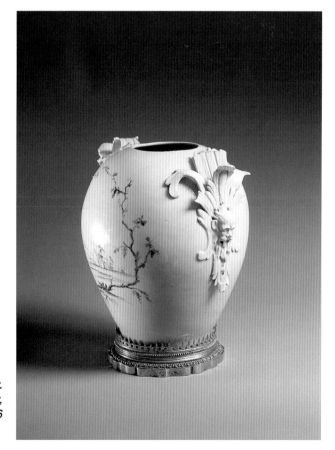

The Divan Room. Vase. By I. G. Miller.
The Imperial Porcelain Factory,
St Petersburg, Russia. After 1756

The Dressing Room. C. van Loo.
"Portrait of Empress Elizabeth Petrovna". 1760

The Dressing Room. Clock and two candelabra.
The Imperial Porcelain Factory,
St Petersburg, Russia. 1846

The Dressing Room.
Mirror in a silver frame
and a toilet set

The Dressing Room.
Unknown Russian painter.
"Portrait of Emperor Peter III".
Between 1770 and 1800

The Dressing Room. The toilet set.
The Imperial Porcelain Factory,
St Petersburg, Russia. 1838

The Dressing Room

23

The Empress's Study.
P. Hackaert. "Neptune's Grotto at Tivoli".
Late 18th century

The Empress's Study.
Lyre-shaped clock.
By J. Birdier. France.
18th century.

The Empress's Study.
Twin vases with
the figures of naiads.
Designed by A. Voronikhin.
The Imperial Porcelain
Factory, St Petersburg,
Russia. 1800s

The Empress's Study

*The Empress's Study.
V. Erichsen. "Portrait
of Catherine the Great"*

*The Empress's Study. G. von Kügelchen. "Portrait
of Empress Maria Fiodorovna in a Funeral Dress". 1801*

*The Empress's Study. Unknown Russian painter. "Portrait
of Emperor Paul I". After J.-L. Voille. 19th century*

*Items of the Etruscan
Service. The Imperial
Porcelain Factory,
St Petersburg, Russia.
1844*

*The Small Passage Room. S. Pulzone.
"Portrait of Vittoria Accoramboni,
a 16th-Century Italian Poet". 1570s*

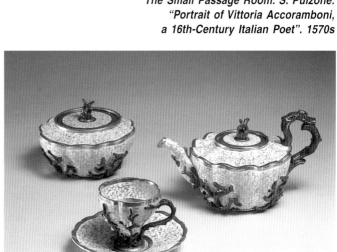

*Items of the Coral Service. The Imperial Porcelain
Factory, St Petersburg, Russia. 1847*

*The Standard Room. Unknown Russian
painter. "Portrait of Empress
Catherine the Great".
After F. Rokotov. 18th century*

◀ *The Standard
Room*

*The Cavaliers-in-
Attendance Room*

The Large Blue Drawing Room

The Large Blue Drawing Room.
L.E. Vigée-Lebrun. "Portrait of Empress
Maria Fiodorovna". 1800s

The Large Blue Drawing Room.
Items from the Banquet Service.
The Imperial Porcelain Factory,
St Petersburg, Russia. 1848–53

◀ The Large Blue Drawing Room. The Banquet
Service. The Imperial Porcelain Factory,
St Petersburg, Russia. 1848–53

The Oak Staircase. B. Coffre. "Portrait of Peter the Great". 1713 or 1716

The Oak Study. Decorative panels with representations of Peter the Great and trophies after drawings by N. Pineau. 1718–20

The Oak Straircase. Architect ▶ J.-B. Le Blond, sculptor N. Pineau

The Oak Study

The Upper Gardens. Pylons of the main gate. Architect B.F. Rastrelli. 1754

C. Kaestner. "Catherine the Great Leaving Peterhof". 1762

The Upper Gardens

Adjoining the Great Palace from the south are the Upper Gardens which play the role of the formal *court-d'honneur*. Its area is 15 hectares. At first the garden was used for economical and engineering purposes – vegetables were grown on beds and the three ponds which were designed to supply the fountain system, were also used for breeding fish. Only in the second half of the eighteenth century this "kitchen garden", as it was then called, became a regular park. It was also during the same period that fountains began to be constructed one after another in this area. Gradually the system of five fountains took its shape in the Upper Gardens, a system which, having changed its decor several times, has basically survived to the present day. In the late eighteenth century the main decorative feature of the park was introduced – the sculptural group *Neptune*, designed by Hans Ritter and Georg Schweigger in the middle of the eighteenth century, was erected in the centre of the large pool.

The Neptune Fountain. 1799

The Oak Fountain.
Architects I. Blank and I. Davydov. 1735

The Lower Park

The terrace in front of the northern façade of the Great Palace affords a splendid view of the Lower Park and the sea. The Great Cascade with its gilded sculptures and the silver of its water jets is glistening in the centre. This is the focal point of the grand fountain system of Peterhof. Its imagery reflects the main idea behind the Peterhof complex – the glorification of outstanding victories of Russia in its struggle for the Baltic shores.

It was not a coincidence that Peter the Great chose this area for his suburban residence. Studying the nearby heights, he found 20 kilometers further to the south of the site several water reservoirs which were fed by springs issuing from the ground. In 1721 a water supply system was built and water began to flow by gravity to the Peterhof storage pools and, when released, rushed down through the pipes and erupted in a great number of water jets in the fountains of the Lower Park.

The composition of the Great Cascade, conceived by Peter himself, was realized by the architects Jean-Baptiste Le Blond and Niccolo Michetti. In Peter's reign the grottos were built, the balustrade erected and the first bas-reliefs and mascarons were made. Twelve allegorical figures and decorative vases and bowls were cast in Holland to decorate the two seven-step cascades.

After the death of Peter the Great, his ideas continued to be implemented – the Basket Fountain was erected in front of the Lower Grotto and over it a group of two tritons trumpeting conches modelled by Carlo Bartolomeo Rastrelli was installed. The centre of the water pool was adorned with the statue of Samson by the same sculptor and it became the main feature of the most powerful fountain of Peterhof.

The decision to erect the Samson Fountain was taken as early as 1734, when the 25th anniversary of the defeat of the Swedish troops at Poltava was celebrated. This memorable event took place on 27 June 1909, the feast day of St Sampsonius, and this fact suggested an idea to create an allegorical representation of the battle as the fight between the biblical hero Samson and a lion. The allegory symbolized Russia's victory over Sweden – the lion is depicted on its coat-of-arms.

Radical changes took place in the decor of the cascade at the very beginning of the nineteenth century, when, on the orders of Paul I, the old lead pieces of sculpture from the Petrine period were replaced with gilded bronze statues. The most eminent sculptors of the period, such as Fedot Shchedrin, Jean-Dominique Rachette, Fiodor Shubin, Ivan Prokofyev, Ivan Martos and Mikhail Kozlovsky took part in this work.

To the right and left of the pool of the Great Cascade are extensive flower parterres with the Bowl Fountains.

They are an important feature in the fountain decoration of the central area of the Lower Park, serving as a compositionally balance to the 20-metre-high water column of the Samson Fountain and articulating the space in front of the Great Cascade.

The pool of the Great Cascade is connected with the sea by a canal which is the north-south axis of Peterhof's ground plan and divides the park into two parts, the eastern and western ones. On either side of the canal, at the crossings of the slant avenues leading from the Great Parterres to the sea in the depth of the park, there are twin fountains, the oldest in Peterhof, which are similarly decorated with sculptures, *Adam* and *Eve*. The sculptures were commissioned by Peter the Great from the Italian sculptor Giovanni Bonazza.

According to Peter the Great's concept, each of the palaces in the Lower Park was to be matched by a fountain cascade. In the eastern part of the park, at the end of the avenue leading from the Palace of Monplaisir to the slope of the terrace, is the Chessboard Hill Cascade. The four huge sloping steps are painted as a chessboard, hence the name of the cascade. The entrance to the upper grotto is guarded by three dragons. Powerful streams of water spout from their open mouths and flow down the steps. Along the sides of the cascade are the marble statues of ancient deities bought by Peter the Great in Italy – *Neptune, Flora, Adonis, Pomona*, etc.

The parterre in front of the Chessboard Hill is decorated with two Roman Fountains erected in 1738–39 by the architects Ivan Blank and Ivan Davydov and rebuilt later by Francesco Bartolomeo Rastrelli. These fountains, hardly not the most magnificent in Peterhof, owe their name to their counterparts on the square in front of St Peter's in Rome.

No less splendid and unusual from the point of view of their technical design are two other fountains in the eastern part of the Lower Park, the Pyramid Fountain and the Sun Fountain.

Peter the Great's attention, while on a visit to France, was caught, among other sights of Versailles, by the fountain looking like a triumphal structure. Later he commissioned Michetti to make a copy of the unusual Versailles fountain. The effect of a water pyramid is achieved through a gradual lessening of the diameters of 505 copper pipes.

The Sun Fountain stands in the middle of a wide reservoir that had formerly served as a bathing-pool. At the top of a rotating pillar set into motion by a water-wheel, are fixed three parallel discs. Each of them has 187 openings. The jets of water spurted out look like rays of sunlight.

The Great Cascade.
The Western Cascade Stairway.
Statue: "Ganymede". 1800.
Copy from a Classical original

The Great Cascade. The Upper Grotto.
Fountain mascaron: "Neptune".
Sculptor C. Rastrelli. 1724

The Great Cascade. The Western
Cascade Stairway. Statue: "Actaeon".
Sculptor I. Martos. 1801

The Great Cascade.
The "Samson Rending
Open the Jaws of
the Lion" Fountain.
Sculptor M. Kozlovsky.
1802

The Pool of the Sea Canal.
Fountain group: "Sirens".
Sculptors F. Shchedrin,
A. Anisimov and
I. Timofeyev. 1805

The Upper Balustrade. Urn-shaped ases. After designs and models by A. Voronikihin and M. Kozlovsky. 1800. Copies from Classical originals

The Great Cascade. The Western Cascade Stairway

41

The Great Cascade. The balustrade of the Upper Grotto.
Decorative vase. After a drawing by A. Voronikhin. 1801

The Great Cascade. The waterfall step.
Low relief: "Perseus Rescuing Andromeda"

The Great Cascade. The waterfall step.
Low relief: "Pan with a Satyr and Cupids"

44

The Great Cascade.
The Eastern Cascade Stairway

The Great Cascade.
The Basket Fountain.
Architect N. Michetti. 1723.
Architect N. Benois. 1860

The Great Fountain ▶
(the Bowl Fountain).
Architect
N. Michetti. 1721–25.
Architect
A. Stakenschneider.
1854

The Danaid Fountain. Architect A. Stackenschneider. 1854.
Sculptor I. Vitali (after C. Rauch's original)

Mascaron. Detail
of the Danaid Fountain

The Adam Fountain.
Architect N. Michetti. 1722.
Sculptor G. Bonazza. 1718

The Eve Fountain.
Architects N. Michetti
and T. Usov. 1726.
Sculptor G. Bonazza. 1718

The Great Orangery. Architect J. Braunstein. 1722–25

The Roman Fountain. Architects I. Blank, I. Davydov. 1738–39. ▶
Architect B.-F. Rastrelli. 1763

The Orangery Triton Fountain.
Architects T. Usov and J.-F. Braunstein.
Sculptor C. Rossi. 1725–26

The Chessboard Hill Cascade. Architects M. Zemtsov,
I. Blank and I. Davydov. 1737–39

Dragon. Detail of the Chessboard Hill Cascade

Trick fountain: "Mushroom"

Trick fountain: "Bench"

Sun Fountain. Architects N. Miketti. 1724.
Architects Y. Velten and I. Yakovlev. 1772–76

*The Golden Hill Cascade. Architect N. Michetti. 1723.
Architect M. Zemtsov. 1732. Architect N. Benois. 1870*

*The Triton Cloche Fountain.
Architect J. Braunstein. 1721*

In the western part of the park is one more cascade, the Golden Hill. Peter the Great made the architect Niccolo Michetti responsible for its construction when the Marly Palace began to be built in the area. The architect made designs strictly in accordance with the Emperor's instructions. The steps of white marble descending from 14-metre height, the golden sheets of the risers, the sculpture of the balustrade, all adds to the unusually magnificent effect of the cascade.

On either side of the Golden Hill Cascade are imposing fountains with powerful jets of water. They are known as the Menazherny (Economical) Fountains. Also built only in the nineteenth century, they were conceived by Peter the Great himself. The fountain is designed so that the huge, seemingly plentiful water shaft is empty inside, hence its name.

It must be mentioned that Peter the Great took an interest not only in technical structures, but in the layout of the park too. Some documents containing his orders as to what kinds of trees were to be planted, how to lay avenues and how to build the drainage system have been preserved. He personally supervised the laying-out of the Venus Garden near the Marly Palace and a small garden southwards of the Palace of Monplaisir.

The focal point of the Monplaisir Garden is the Sheaf Fountain. Four similarly functioning fountains were located at its sides. But especially popular this corner of the Lower Park is for its trick fountains and splendid tulips blossoming each spring and reminding about the founder of this summer residence.

The Palace of Monplaisir

A high artificial terrace, strengthened with huge granite boulders, juts out into the sea. In the eastern part of the Lower Park, behind it, there can be seen a one-storeyed brick building with a pitched roof. This is Peter the Great's favourite palace, Monplaisir. The Tsar himself chose the site for the construction of the palace and sketched the overall composition, the plan of the house and even some details of its decor. The construction, led by the architect Johann Braunstein, begun in 1714 and completed in 1723, when a large festival was held for the first time in Peterhof.

The original plan of the palace was simple: its central volume was occupied by dwelling premises flanked by two galleries with *lusthaus* pavilions. The latter were used to accommodate paintings by Western European artists of the seventeenth and eighteenth centuries. Especially suited for picture displays were the galleries where the wide piers between the windows of the northern wall panelled with oak allowed to hang the paintings in pairs, one below another. The paintings were mainly works by Dutch and Flemish masters – Peter the Great either bought them himself or they were purchased at sales in Amsterdam on his commissions.

The eastern gallery adjoins the Chinese Study which houses a collection of Chinese and Japanese porcelain. The study leads to the main interior of the palace which is known as the Hall. The formal character of this interior intended for receptions is stressed by its huge dimensions and the wealth of its decor. Its walls are lined with oak panelling and adorned with pictures set into the panels. The five representations of ships riding at anchor by Adam Silo are most noteworthy among the paintings. Legend has it that Peter the Great used them to take examinations at the Naval Academy.

But the most prominent feature of the Hall is its dome-shaped rectangular ceiling painted by the French artist Philippe Pillement. Its four facets bear representations of the four elements – *Water, Air, Fire* and *Earth*. At the corners where the facets meet are placed companion sculptural pieces symbolizing the four seasons of the year. And reigning over all this composition is Apollo, the god of poetry, art and the sun. Using a symbolic idiom, the artist wanted to emphasize the eternally changing nature of the world, seasonal changes and the transience of life, in which only art is immortal.

Next to the Hall are the Kitchen, with its walls covered with tiles, which were then brought from the Dutch town of Delft, and the Pantry used for keeping utensils and table-linen. On the fireplace are eight teapots, a present to Peter the Great from the Emperor of China.

To the east of the Hall are the Emperor's private apartments – the Bedchamber and his Maritime Study. Through the windows of the study overlooking the sea he could enjoy a sight of Kronstadt on the one side and St Petersburg on the other. Peter liked this room. By using a telescope, he could watch ships sailing by to the northern capital of Russia or to the West.

The walls in the Bedchamber of Monplaisir, like in all other Peter's palaces, are lined with fabric and the bed has a heavy canopy over it. There visitors can see a gown, a nightcap, a towel and a toilet set, while at the foot of the bed is a Spanish table-top brazier for warming the room. All these things are Peter the Great's personal belongings.

Next to the Bedchamber is the Secretary's Room which is worthy of special mention for the number and quality of paintings hung there. The two marines painted by Adriaen van der Salm in grisaille and depicting ships at roadstead near Archangel and Amsterdam are particularly interesting among the twenty-four pictures kept in this small room. They serve as an evidence of long-standing links between these two port cities.

The Hall

The Hall.
A. Storck.
"A City Pier"

Decorative plate: "Peacock".
Delft, Holland. Ca. 1730

The Kitchen

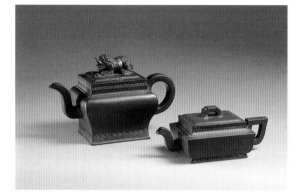

Stoneware teapots.
China. 1662–1722

The Chinese Study

The Bedroom. Toilet set of Peter the Great

The Bedroom. G. Dou. "Food Shop"

The Maritime Study

The Bedroom ▶

60

The Western Gallery. W. van de Velde the Younger.
"Ships Riding Quietly at Anchor"

The Secretary's Room

The Service Galleries of Monplaisir

The Bathhouse Block
The Assembly Hall

Already during the construction of the Dutch House it became clear that it could accommodate only a small number of people. Therefore in 1719–21 Johann Braunstein put up galleries parallel to the façade of the palace and linked them by arches with the *lusthaus* pavilions. The "Family Apartments", as they were called, were intended for guests.

Later, a building with bathing-pools and baths was added to the Monplaisir complex. In the course of the eighteenth century this wing was repeatedly redesigned. In 1856–66 on the site of the former wooden Bathhouse a new stone one was built to the design of the architect Eduard Hahn. In the decor of the façades the architect used some features of the Palace of Monplaisir and retained the layout of the building, the pool with a trick fountain and the steam bath.

Proceeding from the Bathhouse eastwards one could reach the Chinese Garden designed in the landscape style by Eduard Hahn in 1866. Near the Bathhouse stand three buildings projecting one in front of another: the Assembly Hall – the wing attached to Hahn's edifice, the Pantry and the Kitchen with a Coffee Room.

In 1747 Francesco Bartolomeo Rastrelli was ordered to reconstruct the Kitchen Hall into the Assembly Hall. The architect hung there seventeen tapestries woven at the St Petersburg Tapestry Factory in the first half of the eighteenth century. Eight of them, depicting narrative scenes, reproduced the series of the so-called *Tenture des Indes* and had conventional names of the parts of the world – *Asia, America* and *Africa*. the other, narrow ornamental tapestries, were used to cover the piers between windows.

The surviving collection of tapestries has survived and now adorns the walls of the Assembly Hall which has opened after restoration.

The Catherine Block

In 1748–49 Rastrelli erected, on the undercroft of the orangery, which was part of the auxiliary structures of Monplaisir, a stone palace which was larger in dimensions and volume than the Dutch House. However, the original Baroque decor of the interiors of the building existed for less than thirty years. Already in 1785–86 it was completely redesigned by the Italian architect Giacomo Quarenghi. Some alterations in the decor of the rooms were made in the first decades of the nineteenth century.

The main decorative elements in the majority of the rooms are Classical mouldings, Empire-style painting in grisaille, single-tone painted decoration of the walls and the smooth ceiling. In some of the rooms mid-eighteenth century stoves have been preserved.

The collection of the Catherine Block is made up of a superb set of Russian furniture produced in the late eighteenth century and in the first three decades of the nineteenth. Associated with this kind of decorative art are such glorious names as Andrei Voronikhin, Vasily Stasov and Carlo Rossi. Visitors to the palace are usually overwhelmed by superb bronzes, candelabra and incense-burners pro-

duced by French craftsmen, as well as porcelain made at the Imperial Porcelain Factory in St Petersburg, which was quite on a par with the the products of the most famous factories of Europe.

The main feature of the Catherine Block is the Guryev Service which decorates the huge table in the Yellow Hall. This is one of the most luxurious and famous services of the factory. It was commissioned for the Emperor Alexander I in 1809 by Count Dmitry Guryev, hence its name. Originally the service was known as the "Russian" one – the decor of the set was a kind of encyclopaedia of Russia. Its plates were adorned with representations of the numerous peoples of Russia and various popular types of the huge country. For this purpose drawings from such books as *St Petersburg Scenes and Types* by Christian Geissler and *The Peoples of Russia* by Johann Georgi were used. The compositions of the three-dimensional pieces included sculptural groups of young lads and girls in Russian national costumes.

From the reign of Catherine the Great the building was the venue for formal dinners and annual balls in honour of the graduates of the Smolny Institute for Noble Girls.

The Green Reception Room

The Bedroom of Alexander I

The Study of Alexander I. Unknown Russian artist.
"Portrait of Emperor Paul I". Between 1770 and 1800.
After A. Roslin

The Anteroom

The Study of Alexander I

The Blue Reception Room

The Babigon Service. Plate with a view of the terrace in front of the Palace of Monplaisir. The Imperial Porcelain Factory, St Petersburg, Russia. 1823–24

The Yellow Hall. G. Dawe. "Portrait of Empreror Alexander I". 1825

Porcelain sculptures from the series "Street Craftsmen and Vendors" by J.D. Rachette. The Imperial Porcelain Factory, St Petersburg, Russia. 1770s–1780s

Items from the Guryev Service.
The Imperial Porcelain Factory,
St Petersburg, Russia. 1809–17

The Yellow Hall. Unknown artist. "Portrait
of Catherine the Great". Copy from a painting
by J.-B. Lampi the Elder. Early 19th century

The Yellow Hall. The Guryev Service. The Imperial
Porcelain Factory, St Petersburg, Russia. 1809–17

The Yellow Hall ▶

The Hermitage

In the depth of the Lower Park, on the seashore, there stands an elegant two-storey edifice – the first Russia's Hermitage built by the architect Johann Friedrich Braunstein in 1721–25. Its particular impression of lightness and elegance is due to the large windows and metal openwork railings of elaborate design. The building is enclosed with a deep moat which is spanned by a light bridge.

The idea of building the Hermitage came to Peter the Great during his travels in Europe where such pavilions were then fashionable. But the initiator of the construction had no opportunity to see the pavilion completed – the work finished only in the summer of 1725, already after Peter's death.

The first storey of the pavilion is occupied by the Pantry and the Kitchen where dishes were warmed before being served. In the eighteenth century the upper floor could be reached only in a special chair-lift for two persons which was hoisted by a winch. This lift of a kind was in good working order until 1797, when, during a visit by Paul I and his family to the the Hermitage, the mechanism broke down and the members of the family could be evacuated only with the help of a ladder. The Emperor ordered to destroy the lifting mechanism and the present-day inner staircase was then built.

The upper storey of the Hermitage is a vast Hall full of light and air. It was precisely for the sake of this vast interior that the whole building was erected. The Hall was intended for a narrow circle of the owner's most intimate friends who used to gather here. Fourteen people could sit in the centre of the room around the oval table with covers laid in front of each of them. The central section

of the table with serving dishes was lifted from below through a special shaft, as described above. Any participant in the feast, however, could order a meal of his own. To this end, he was to state his wish in a note, put it on the plate and pull the string. Downstairs, in the Pantry, the bell rang and the servants lowered the plate through the shaft. A little later the plate with the ordered meal was sent back upstairs.

The main decoration of the Hall are 124 paintings by Western European artists bought on commissions from Peter the Great. The pictures include battle scenes by Jacques Courtois, called Le Burguignon, the most popular battle painter of the eighteenth century, still lifes by the French painter Jean Louis Prevost, sea views by the Dutch artists Micheel Maddersteeg and Ludolf Backhuyzen, the representations of the Apostles by the Dutch artist Georg Gsell, who was invited by Peter the Great to serve in Russia and spent 23 years in this country. No less interesting are works by Italian artists, such as *Apollo and Marsyas* by Gasparo Carpioni, *Antiochus and Stratonica* by Gasparo Dizziani and *The Death of Cato* by Giovanni Battista Longhetti. The shield of the fireplace is decorated with a large-scale painting, *Diogenes' Drinking Cup*, by the Dutch artist Nicolaes Rosendael. The only work in the Hermitage collection produced in Russia is *The Battle of Poltava,* painted by an anonymous Russian master in the eighteenth century.

A small but representative and diverse collection of the Hermitage allows the visitor not only to see the world through the eyes of the artists of the seventeenth and eighteenth centuries, but also to have some idea about the collecting of the fine arts in Russia during that period.

The Hall. G. de Lairesse. "Anthony and Cleopatra"

The Hall. G. Gsell. "The Apostle Paul"

The Hall

The Hall. G. Berckheyde.
"City Street"

The Hall. J.M. Molenaer.
"Village Wedding"

The Hall. G. Diziani.
"Antiochus and Stratonica"

The Hall. Unknown Russian artist.
"The Battle of Poltava".
First half of the 18th century

The Hall. Jugs. Ansbach, Germany.
Delft, Holland. First half of the 18th century

Decorative plate:
"Peacock". Delft, Holland.
Ca. 1730

The Kitchen

The Marly Palace

Another palace of the Petrine Age, the Marly, is located in the western part of the Lower Park, between two ponds. It was built to the design of the architect Johann Friedrich Braunstein in 1720–24. The palace owed its name to the residence of the French kings, Marly-le Roi near Paris. This small two-storey building plays an important part in the layout of the park. Three main avenues, the central Marly Avenue, the northern Maliebaan Alley and the southern Birch Walk, diverge from it.

Rapid construction work began in this area with the building of two ponds, the rectangular Marly Pond, and the semicircular one, divided into four sections, known as the Sectorial Ponds. The excavated soil was used to raise a huge rampart along the sea gulf, which served both as a dam and as a barrier protecting the palace from northern winds. In addition to aesthetic purposes, these artificial water reservoirs were used for economical aims too – for keeping fish.

The Marly Palace is unusual in design – it has no traditional state hall. A long corridor extends from the Entrance Hall with its doors leading to the living premises and auxiliary rooms. On the ground floor, one side is occupied by the Pantry and the Kitchen, with tableware, utensils and vessels from the seventeenth and eighteenth centuries. On the other side are the Bedroom, the Duty Room and the Plane Study where the Emperor's surviving personal belongings are kept. It was to the Entrance Hall that Peter the Great accorded the role of a state room.

All living rooms in the palace are decorated with paintings by Western European artists. Paintings invariably played an important role in the embellishment of interiors in Peter's palaces. The major part of the paintings kept in the Marly Palace has survived to this day. The collection includes works by Dutch, Flemish and Italian artists such as Adam Silo, Abraham Storck, Alexander Grevenbroeck, Peeter Neeffs the Elder, Pietro Belotti and Andrea Celesti.

The staircase leads to the upper floor. Its steps are made of oak. The railings of burnished steel are decorated with a gilded floral ornament and Peter the Great's emblem under the crown. The magnificent, finely wrought railings are the work of Nicolas Pineau.

The seven rooms of the upper storey also served as the Tsar's private apartments. Once the Marly Palace was the main repository of Peter the Great's wardrobe. Later the major part of the collection was transferred for storage to the Imperial Hermitage Museum in St Petersburg. But even those items of clothing which remain in the Wardrobe Room and the Dressing Room may be regarded as precious relics of the Petrine Age. The most significant exhibits on display are the Tsar's naval greatcoat, his kaftan with the embroidered badge of the Order of St Andrew the First-Called and the white camisole embroidered with a single-toned pattern.

The table with a slate blackboard produced by Peter the Great himself and preserved in the Oak Study is also a valuable object in the Marly collection. In the quiet, homely atmosphere of this small apartment one could eagerly engage in reading or thinking, which is suggested by the open volumes on the beautiful inlaid bureau of Italian work and by books in the Emperor's library that is opposite the Study. The thematic range of Peter's collection of books gives an idea of his tastes and interests.

The Entrance Hall. A. Celesti. "Christ and the Samaritan Woman"

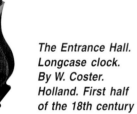

The Entrance Hall.
Longcase clock.
By W. Coster.
Holland. First half
of the 18th century

The Library

The Entrance Hall

The Plane Study. Bureau. Italy. Late 17th century

The Duty Room. Rinse Verzyll. "Morning"

The Dining Room

The Pantry

The Dressing Room. Cupboard.
South Germany. Early 18th century

The Corner Room.
Albarelli (pharmacy vessels).
Italy. Mid-18th century

The Kitchen

The Cottage Palace

The landscaped Alexandria Park with the Cottage Palace, where everything bespeaks calm and silence, is situated to the south-east of the formal Lower Park with its noise and glamour. Alexandria was conceived as a private Imperial country estate. Emperor Nicholas I presented it to his wife Alexandra, hence the name of the estate.

In keeping with the owners' wishes, all the structures in Alexandria were to be executed in the Gothic style. Therefore, the architect Adam Menelaws, who built the Cottage, used the elements of the English or Tudor Gothic style. The palace strikes visitors by the harmony of its interior decoration marked by an unusual artistic integrity and authenticity.

The most richly adorned are the rooms on the ground floor, the private apartments of the Empress – the Study, the Drawing Room, the Large and Small Reception Rooms and the Dining Room. The moulded ceilings, the fine carving on the door and window surrounds, the grisaille painting of the stoves, the marble fireplaces, the furniture, the carpets on the floor – all these elements strikingly combine luxury and cosiness. The palace houses a vast collection of works of applied art produced during the so-called "Historicism" period in the nineteenth century.

Of particular importance in the interior decor of the Cottage is its furniture created after drawings by Menelaws in the "Gothic" taste and produced of ash-wood, oak, walnut and maple by the famous court cabinet-maker Heinrich Gambs.

A huge Gothic bookcase extends along the entire length of a wall in the library. The collection of books amounted to over 1000 volumes, mainly works of fiction in German, French and English. A place of honour was given to the multivolume *Collection of the Laws of the Russian Empire*, the beloved creation of Nicholas I.

The Dining Room is particularly impressive. The large formal table laid for 24 persons with His Majesty's Own Service was manufactured at the Imperial Porcelain Factory in St Petersburg specially for the Cottage Palace. Each of its pieces is decorated with the coat-of arms of Alexandria – a sword in a wreath of roses on a blue ground and the motto: "For God, Tsar and the Motherland". The coat-of-arms, created by the poet Vasily Zhukovsky, the tutor of the Emperor's children, is also present in the decor of the façades and interiors of the Cottage, as well as on the other structures in the park. A set of crystal pieces and articles of coloured glass add to the wealth of the table decoration.

The collection of painting in the Cottage, unlike the other Peterhof palaces, consists mainly of works by outstanding Russian painters, such as Ivan Aivazovsky, Orest Kiprensky, Sylvester Shchedrin, Maxim Vorobyev and Pimen Orlov.

Some exhibits in the Palace are not only of a significant artistic value, but also have a great historical significance. For example, beautiful companion vases produced at the Sèvres Factory in 1800 and presented by Napoleon Bonaparte to Emperor Alexander I during the conclusion of the Tilsit Treaty in 1807 are noteworthy.

The fine wrought-iron staircase with its walls painted from top to bottom in grisaille connects all the three storeys of the Cottage. The beautiful painted decoration of the staircase, creating an illusion of soaring Gothic pillars and arches, was executed by the artist Giovanni Scotti.

The embellishment of the first floor is much more modest and austere. Located there were the rooms of the children and Nicholas I, the Dressing Room and the Study with a collection of Dutch painting from the seventeenth and early eighteenth centuries. The only exclusion is an ornate study in the Art Nouveau style which was decorated in the late nineteenth century and belonged to the widow Empress Maria Fiodorovna, the last Tsar's mother.

Incidentally, Nicholas II also used Alexandria as his country residence until 1914. The so-called Lower Dacha built for him on the shore of the Gulf of Finland has not survived.

The Drawing Room. Y. Botman. "Portrait
of the Empreror Nicholas I". 1849

The Study. V. Gau. "Portrait of Empress
Alexandra Fiodorovna". 1834

*E. Gau. "The Drawing Room
of the Cottage Palace". 1861*

*The Drawing Room of Alexandra
Fiodorovna. Clock: "Rouen Cathedral".
The Imperial Porcelain Factory.
St Petersburg. Russia. 1830*

*The Dining Room. Items of Her Majesty's Own Service.
The Imperial Porcelain and Glass Factories,
St Petersburg, Russia. Late 1820s – early 1830s*

The Library

◄ *The Dining Room*

A. Benois. "The Maids-of-Honours Blocks". 1900

The Benois Family Museum

Not far from the Great Palace, on the south-eastern border of the square in front of the Church Block, there stand two similar two-storey buildings, known as the Maids-of-Honour Blocks. They were built to the plans of Nikolai Benois, Court Architect to Emperor Nicholas I, in 1858. The decor of the façades, apparently modelled on eighteenth-century examples, was explained by the proximity of Rastrelli's Great Palace. The Maids-of-Honour Blocks were intended for the accommodation of those members of the court who accompanied the Imperial family to Peterhof for the summers.

In 1988 one of the blocks was converted into a museum of the Benois family. It occupies a special place in the complex of the Peterhof museums. The museum is unique even among artistic collections of the country. Amassed there are works by several generations of one family, but its artistic scope was so great that visitors to the museum have a rare opportunity to acquaint themselves with an extremely wide range of Russian and European cultural phenomena from the nineteenth and twentieth centuries.

The idea to build up the museum belonged to Nikolai Benois, son of the well-known artist and scholar Alexander Benois. Nikolai Benois is an outstanding theatrical artist whose name is associated with the revival of the famous Italian La Scala Theatre during the post-war years. He succeeded in uniting the efforts of the members of the Benois family living in various countries of Europe, America and in Russia, as well as of numerous art collectors, museum workers and of all those who contributed to this project, which resulted in the creation of a new magnificent artistic collection at Peterhof.

During the Second World War practically all the palaces and parks of Peterhof suffered heavy damage. It took decades of strenuous efforts of many hundreds of restorers to return its former splendour and its glory of the summertime capital of Russia to this masterpiece of palace-and-park art of the eighteenth and nineteenth centuries.

In summertime, the Palaces are open from 10.30 a.m. to 18 p.m.
Visitors are admitted until 17 p.m.
The Great Palace, the Hermitage Palace, the Marly Palace, the Cottage Palace
and the Museum of the Benois Family are open daily, except Mondays.
The Monplaisir Palace and The Bathhouse Block Museum are open daily, except Wednesdays.
The Catherine Block Museum is open daily, except Thursdays.

The Lower Park is open daily from 9 a.m. to 20 p.m.
The fountains are functioning from 11 a.m. to 17 p.m.